FROM THE
CRADLE
TO THE
PRESENT

WILLIAM EPPS JR.

Printed in the United States of America

ISBN 979-8-89114-083-7 (hc)
ISBN 979-8-89114-082-0 (sc)
ISBN 979-8-89114-084-4 (e)

Library of Congress Control Number: 2024904062

2024.04.30

MainSpring Books
5901 W. Century Blvd
Suite 750
Los Angeles, CA, US, 90045

www.mainspringbooks.com

FROM THE CRADLE TO THE PRESENT

I had no clue of what was going on at the cradle. However, as time progressed, my knowledge began to open up that I wanted to know what was beyond my neck of the woods, thus I became more aware of what I needed to know.

I started school and it was all a great opportunity to begin to comprehend such a task. I still want to know more about the who, what, where when, how and the why. I was like a sponge, just soaking it all up. It's known to be the truth; the mind is to pressure to waste on nothing.

I wanted to obtain as much knowledge as I could. While in grade school I was doing some artwork for the school. When I was in high school, I continued artwork. My teachers told me to continue art school. After high school, I enrolled at Virginia Union University where I received an Associate Degree in Christian Education. Following this, I joined the United States Marine Corps. After my service, I enrolled at Andersonville Baptist Seminary. At Andersonville, I earned both a Bachelor's and Master's Degree in Biblical Studies, and subsequently obtained a Doctorate in Christian Education. Additionally, I pursued art studies through home art classes, earning a certificate.

During this time, I balanced my studies with teaching Christian Education, maintaining a busy schedule.

I wanted to learn how to fly airplanes, so I completed flight school. Subsequently, I operated three trucks on the road. There was a lot on my bucket list but I persevered without giving up. As the old saying goes, "Quitters never win, but winners never quit." I have traveled to many countries just to see what the world looks like from a different view. I still have a lot on my bucket list to do. Never let anything come between you and your state of mind. Never put off today for tomorrow, because there's no tomorrow.

Life's challenges may thrust you into unfamiliar territory, but stand tall, face them head-on, and persevere. I find great depth in the history of the Old Testament, with its invaluable lessons. The Old Testament lays the groundwork, while the New Testament builds upon it, pointing to the completion of God's work through Jesus on the cross, offering salvation.

Some believe that God owes them something, but in truth, it was Jesus's sacrifice on Calvary that grants us freedom from sin. Satan seeks to bring us down, but Jesus paid a steep price for our salvation. I find myself caught between sin and salvation, with Jesus's sacrifice as my anchor.

Satan is not to be trusted. He will turn out the lights on you because he is the prince of darkness. The ruler of darkness in high places, Satan needs no light because light will put him out of business. However, he is trying to pull the wool over your eyes, and body slam you for the count. Never take this guy lightly, because he is a force to be reckoned with.

If Satan stands toe to toe with Jesus, what are we to him? We simply put the word on him. Call upon Jesus. This word is too heavy for him to carry. This reminds me of a story about an old man and a young man. The old man symbolizes Wisdom; he knows how to carry it but cannot run with it. The young man is strong and can run with it but lacks the wisdom to carry it properly. We must teach young people the ways of Wisdom so that when they encounter Satan, they don't falter. Satan doesn't bring out just any weapon; he brings out heavy artillery. He knows the what, where, when, and how.

Let's consider the presentation: the Old Testament forms the foundation, while the New Testament builds upon it. They are interrelated, with the New Testament contained within the Old. The Old Testament lays the groundwork, while the New Testament provides explanations. Together, they form a divine library—a seamless unity connecting past origins to future destinies, bridging two eternities.

It's intriguing to note Ezra 7:21, where the Hebrew alphabet lacks the letter J, a letter the Gentiles could pronounce—a potential miracle. Reflecting on Genesis 4:15, where God marked Cain, we see the first evidence of God's written communication. From Genesis 1 to 11, we witness the creation of Adam leading to the Tower of Babel—a narrative of man's attempt at a worldwide empire.

God's call to Abraham in Genesis 12 to 38 establishes him as the father of many nations. In Genesis 39 to 50, Isaac's family descends into Egypt, closing out Genesis with Joseph's burial. The Old Testament is a treasure trove of history, each book intricately connected to the others, providing a rhythmic clue to the next. Deuteronomy, for instance, showcases Moses delivering three addresses while in the wilderness.

The first address of Moses reflects on their journey from where they started—an intended 11-day march that extended into a 40-year odyssey. In his second address, Moses expresses gratitude to God for leading them into a new land, emphasizing that disobedience would prevent their entry. The third address focuses on future blessings, contingent upon obedience to God's commands. Canaan, or the Promised Land, spans approximately 180 miles in length and 40 miles in width, serving as the epicenter of civilization and ancient history.

Situated amidst significant historical cities—Egypt, Nineveh, Babylon, Persia, Greece, and Rome—the Holy Land bears the mark of God's sovereignty.

The Book of Judges portrays a tumultuous period known as the dark ages, marked by the abandonment of God and subsequent divine forsaking of the people. Judges are categorized into three types: warrior judges like Gideon and Samson, priestly judges like Eli, and prophet judges like Samuel.

In First Samuel, human choice dictates Saul's kingship, while Second Samuel portrays God's selection of David as king. First Kings details Solomon's reign and Israel's affairs, while Second Kings encompasses the entirety of Israel's monarchy.

First Chronicles examines Solomon's construction of the Temple and the bloodshed in David's lineage, preventing him from building it. Second Chronicles delves into the kings and the Temple's significance, tracing the origins of royal history from Second Samuel.

First Samuel documents the failure of man's king, Saul, while Second Samuel chronicles the enthronement of God's chosen king, David, establishing the lineage from which the Messiah, Jesus Christ, will emerge.

God called David from tending sheep, granting him victory over Goliath despite facing persecution from Saul. David eventually became king over Judah and later over all of Israel. Similarly, God promises to make us kings if we heed His Word rather than relying on our own understanding.

Disregarding God's voice can lead to disastrous outcomes, as evidenced by Adam's disobedience and the subsequent descent into chaos.

Despite life's challenges, we can find solace in the assurance that Jesus will never abandon us. Through the years, God has guided me from darkness into light, providing clarity during uncertain times. Instead of succumbing to despair, I pressed forward, determined to discover my purpose. Satan may tempt us to give up, but by persevering, we gain clarity and purpose.

In my youth, I aspired to fly planes, a dream I achieved through dedication and perseverance. Mastering flight brought immense satisfaction and remains a cherished accomplishment. I also long to sail a yacht again, relishing the freedom and adventure it offers. Despite past setbacks, I remain optimistic about future opportunities to pursue these passions.

In my younger years, I was into drag racing. I spent a lot of money on really fast cars. But now, beyond adrenaline-fueled pursuits, I now focus on writing and artwork, alongside enriching travels across the globe. Exploring new cultures and landscapes expands my horizons and deepens my understanding of the world.

On my bucket list are visits to Senegal and Ghana, alongside revisiting other memorable destinations. As the saying goes, true learning occurs beyond the confines of home, motivating me to continue exploring and growing.

I prioritize keeping my mind sharp by engaging in educational pursuits, as they say, "iron sharpens iron." When we focus on positive endeavors, we become more attuned to recognizing Satan's deceitful schemes.

I find fulfillment in my current endeavors with my books and artwork. I've always believed in striving for success, knowing that failure only occurs if we don't attempt something. Throughout my academic journey, I've made continuous efforts to learn and grow. It's been suggested that we only utilize a fraction of our brain's capacity in a lifetime—an intriguing notion indeed. I can honestly say I'm on a path of personal growth, awaiting guidance from the Master on my next steps. By remaining attentive and receptive to divine direction, we can trust that God will provide for our needs.

I take comfort in the assurance that the righteous are never abandoned, and their descendants never beg for sustenance. In my youth, I sought new horizons and embarked on journeys to explore what lay beyond, even heading westward as some advised. I then developed a curiosity to explore the North, East, and South. Having toured the lower forty-eight states, I now cherish memories of places I'd like to revisit.

I aspire to follow in the footsteps of Abraham and Elijah, mindful of the adage: "Be careful what you wish for, for it might come to pass." In my youth, I resisted the Lord's calling, akin to Jonah fleeing from his destiny, only to find that the Lord's will ultimately prevails.

One unforgettable night, after a powerful encounter, I received a vision of three men in black discussing a divine plan at the foot of my bed, emphasizing the guidance of the Holy Spirit. United as one, they bestowed upon me the Spirit, prompting my fervent response to serve the Lord. Despite facing adversities and Satan's attacks, I stand firm in my faith, refusing to yield. Resilience, not speed or strength, determines victory in the race of life.

Reflecting on ancient texts like the Book of Job, I see God's wisdom in our trials, using them to refine us like gold. Just as Job was broken down, melted, and softened, we too must submit to God's transformative touch. Invoking the Spirit of the Living God, I surrender to His molding, seeking to radiate His love and light. Yet, I remain aware that even in doing good, Satan may seek to undermine our efforts.

In the prophetic book of Isaiah, salvation is the central theme, reflecting God's plan for redemption. Isaiah's very name signifies "Salvation of Jehovah," underscoring the importance of salvation in God's message to His people. As we navigate the challenges of life, let us embrace God's wisdom and grace, trusting in His ultimate plan for our salvation and redemption.

There are seventeen prophetic books in the Old Testament, divided into Major and Minor Prophets. The Southern Kingdom, Judah, features prominently in the themes of these prophets. Fearless and unwavering, the prophets of old condemned the sins of their time, calling people to turn away from idols and back to God. They addressed both moral and political corruption within the nation.

Christ's affirmation of the prophets in Luke 24:25-27 underscores the precision of prophecies regarding Him, affirming the Bible as the Word of God. Through the prophets, God granted glimpses into the distant future. The book of Isaiah presents two distinct messages, serving as a microcosm of the Bible itself with its sixty-six chapters. The first section portrays Israel, while the latter sections focus on Jesus bearing our sins. Isaiah's ministry spanned the reigns of four kings, beginning with King Uzziah. His commission came in the year of Uzziah's death, marked by a profound vision of the Lord in the temple. The book of Isaiah reveals a pattern of nations falling due to moral decay, but also offers hope with its sections on the restoration of Judah.

I've often pondered what it would be like to possess the knowledge of the prophets, praying for God to grant me insight and boldness to stand for Him in a world in need of

His truth. As God asked Isaiah, "Whom shall I send, and who will go for us?" I pray to God to prepare me for the work He has assigned me, ensuring I remain receptive to His guidance amidst any challenges.

I seek the wisdom of God to grasp the mysteries of past, present, and future revelations, akin to Daniel's vision. Though Daniel glimpsed the future, he didn't fully comprehend it, as God instructed him to seal the prophecies for a later time.

Daniel's writings, intended for future generations, provide insights into the coming of Jesus Christ and serve as a beacon of light guiding us towards heaven. God empowers each person to illuminate the path to salvation through the cross. Daniel, a prophet of God, unveiled the future's hidden aspects, showcasing God's power and universal sovereignty. His book offers profound insights for Christian living and devotion. In heaven, Daniel is honored as greatly beloved by God, demonstrating the profound impact of his faithful service. Divided into historical narratives and prophetic revelations, the book of Daniel offers a comprehensive view of future events, often referred to as the ABC of prophecy.

God's Word serves as a mirror, revealing our flaws and guiding us towards correction. At times, our sins may obscure the path to redemption, but God's guidance offers clarity and direction.

We encounter grace both in the Old Testament and the New. Hosea 14:4 speaks of healing for backsliders, highlighting God's ability to provide the right remedy at the right time.

In Joel, spiritual promises concerning the Lord's earthly life and future reign are foretold. Acts 2:16, fulfilled at Pentecost by Peter, offers a lesson applicable to today's church, which may find itself in a desolate state, requiring prayer for revival.

The Gospel of Luke serves as a perpetual guide for the church until Jesus' return. I've always desired to delve deeply into the history of Egypt and Hebrew studies, each offering millennia of research material. The vastness of these studies ensures that one's mind will never be overwhelmed; even a lifetime on Earth barely scratches the surface of the brain's potential.

Maintaining mental acuity is crucial, as idle minds tend to stagnate. Regular engagement with scripture keeps the mind alert and responsive, providing answers for various situations. God has endowed each person with the capacity to observe, listen, and respond appropriately.

Dreamers expand their horizons, while those who remain stagnant risk withering away. It's essential to keep the mind active, as idleness invites Satan's influence, convincing individuals that impending doom is imminent.

Satan, self-proclaimed prince of darkness, is a cunning adversary who prowls about, seeking whom he may devour. He is a formidable foe but turning away from him ensures his power remains ineffective. Being praised and deceived simultaneously can lead to a sudden halt and darkness. How can one blind person describe sight to another if they've never experienced it themselves? It's a humorous notion, but it's crucial not to be caught off guard in Satan's domain, where mercy is scarce.

In Matthew's Gospel, Christ is presented as King, with the first 17 verses detailing His royal genealogy, tracing back to Abraham and David. Mark's Gospel lacks a genealogy, while Luke's traces back to Adam. John's Gospel, though lacking a genealogy, begins with profound significance: "In the beginning was the Word, and the Word was with God, and the Word was God."

The Gospels conclude with distinct endings: Matthew with Jesus commissioning His disciples, Mark with the disciples preaching everywhere, Luke emphasizing Jesus as the perfect man, and John highlighting the countless significant acts of Jesus that the world couldn't contain in books.

Matthew's Gospel serves a particular purpose, demonstrating to the Jews that Jesus is the long-awaited Messiah. Matthew, well-versed in Jewish history and customs, bridges the gap between the Old Testament and the birth of Christ, breaking the 400 years of silence after Malachi's prophecy. It's tailored for a Jewish audience, serving as the 40th book in the Bible—a number symbolizing testing, seen in Jesus' 40-day temptation, Israel's 40 years in the wilderness, and the significant periods in the lives of David and Moses.

We gain insight into Mark's writings, focusing on portraying Jesus Christ as the servant of God. Mark's objective, as seen in Mark 10:45, was to emphasize Christ's role as a servant who came to minister and offer His life as a ransom for many.

Rather than aiming to prove specific statements and prophecies about Jesus, Mark sought to clearly depict certain facts about Him. His Gospel, the shortest at 16 chapters, presents Christ as a humble yet perfect servant of Jehovah.

In contrast, Matthew's 28 chapters portray Christ as the Son of David with kingly dignity. The Gospel opens with John the Baptist preparing the way for the coming Messiah, fulfilling Messianic prophecies.

Mark 1:2 quotes from Malachi 3:1, and verse 4 refers back to Isaiah 40:3, highlighting John's message of preparing a straight highway. Throughout Mark's Gospel, an unbroken service of Christ is recorded, reflecting His mission to teach, comfort, heal, liberate, forgive, and cleanse those in need.

Mark also records Christ's profound statements regarding the Sabbath, emphasizing its purpose to benefit and bless humanity rather than burden them. For instance, in Mark 3:1-5, Jesus responds to questions about Sabbath observance with an illustrative example. The conclusion drawn is that whatever benefits humanity is appropriate for the Sabbath, aligning perfectly with God's intention for the day. Seven of Jesus' recorded miracles occurred on the Sabbath.

The Sabbath, a divine gift to humanity, is emphasized in Mark's Gospel. Following a day of preaching and healing, Jesus rose early the next morning and withdrew to a solitary place for prayer (Mark 1:37-39). The parable of the sower, found in Mark 4:3-20, illustrates the Gospel taking root in the heart, with its interpretation provided in Mark 4:13-20. A parable serves as an analogy, juxtaposing higher truths with earthly examples. After explaining the parables, Jesus and his disciples encountered a storm on the Sea of Galilee, prompting Jesus to calm the tempest with three words: "Peace, be still." This episode marks another instance of Jesus' miraculous power.

In Mark 13, Jesus discloses future events to his troubled disciples in the Olivet discourse, addressing the end of the age, the great tribulation, and the promise of his return. Luke's Gospel portrays Jesus as the perfect man, particularly appealing to the Greeks and sinners. It showcases Christ's compassionate love in his incarnation to save humanity, emphasizing his humanity as well as his divine nature.

Luke's Gospel is poetic in nature, commencing and concluding with songs of praise and blessing to God. It uniquely provides Jesus' genealogy at the time of his baptism, connecting him to both the royal lineage of David through Joseph and his lineage through Mary, tracing back to Adam, the father of humanity. In John 1:1, the author establishes the Word of God, delineating the purpose of his book in the opening eighteen verses, known as the Prologue. John's intent was to demonstrate that Jesus was the promised Messiah for the Jews and the Son of God for the Gentiles.

His primary objective was to guide believers into a divine friendship with Jesus, emphasizing the significance of belief, which is mentioned 98 times in the book. The overarching theme of John's Gospel is the deity of Jesus Christ, portraying the Babe of Bethlehem as the begotten of the Father. Jesus' titles are significant, including the Word, the Creator, the Lamb of God, and the Great I AM (Exodus 3:14). John's Gospel elevates Christ to a higher level compared to the other Gospels, emphasizing spiritual relationships with heavenly beings rather than earthly ones.

While Matthew and Luke depict Jesus as the Son of David and Son of Man, linking him to the Earth, John portrays him as the Son of God, connecting him to the Father in Heaven. In John, Jesus is depicted as dwelling with God before the creation of any creature (John 1:1-2), emphasizing his intimate relationship with the Father.

Throughout John's Gospel, Jesus refers to God as "My Father" 35 times, and his use of "Verily, verily" 25 times underscores his authority. Three keys unlock the message of John's Gospel, with the first key accessible to every child, symbolizing its accessibility and importance.

As many receive him are given power to become the sons of God. The second key unlocks the entire book, stating the Gospel's purpose. Another key, at the last supper with his disciples, Jesus reveals the truth.

John transitioned from New Jerusalem to the Old Testament to meet Moses and engage in conversation. Both men were well-versed in the Old and New Testaments. John understood the Old Testament as the fulfillment of the New Testament, while Moses knew that the New Testament would fulfill what was foretold. The Gospel depicts what Christ began to do, while Acts shows what He continued to do through the Holy Spirit. The Gospel presents Christ's teachings, while Acts illustrates their impact on the actions of the apostles.

Moses and John shared similarities: Moses looked into the future through the front door and saw New Jerusalem, witnessing Jesus' mercy, while John looked back through the back door and saw God's grace for Adam. Moses headed toward New Jerusalem via dry ground, while John was directed toward the Old through water. John observed the fourfold grace extended to Adam: questioning, promise of clothing, promise of salvation, and expulsion from the garden.

The concept of the cross was foreshadowed throughout the Old Testament, but it found its culmination in the New Testament on the hill called Calvary, where the finished work was accomplished. The Old Testament represents God's promises to humanity before the Son came, while the New Testament calls us to believe in the Son.

In the Old Testament, God blessed everyone as a collective group, but through Jesus, blessings are offered on a personal, one-to-one basis. I am grateful that I don't need someone to stand in for me to receive blessings; Jesus made that possible on Calvary. Without Jesus' sacrifice on the cross, there wouldn't be enough animals today to cover humanity's sins.

It would indeed be a dark day if Jesus hadn't paid the price for us. We should express our gratitude and shout, "Thank you, Lord, for doing this for me, a sinner like me."

Let's examine Acts 1 through 12, where Peter urges the Jews to repent, while in Acts 13 through 28, Paul encourages the Gentiles to believe. At Pentecost, the Holy Spirit descended upon the people, leading to the establishment of the first church in Jerusalem, which gained 3000 members on that day.

It's remarkable to see 3000 members gathered in one day, especially when compared to the difficulty of assembling even three people today. They spread their message in Judea, Samaria, and the farthest reaches.

In Romans, the essence of the Gospel is succinctly expressed: Christ is the power of the Gospel, bringing salvation to everyone who believes. The plan is simple: believe and live by faith. The book outlines the consequences of sin and the rewards of righteousness, with Christ serving as the pathway to salvation. Romans paints a courtroom scene, with God as the judge, summoning both Jew and Gentile before Him. The general charge is that all are under sin, and despite their protestations of innocence, the verdict is clear: all are guilty before God.

In John 3:16, the judge asks on whether there is anyone representing the prisoners. Then Jesus says, "Yes, I am here to represent them on the cross."

The first three chapters of Romans paint a stark picture of sin, defining it as falling short or missing the mark. Paul illustrates justification by faith through the example of Abraham in the Old Testament, where faith was counted as righteousness. Abraham received three blessings through his faith: righteousness, inheritance, and posterity.

The Epistle of Galatians emphasizes that believers are no longer under the law but are saved by faith alone. In Romans, we discover our standing, while in Galatians, we take our stand. In Romans, we use our intellect to understand the core tenets of Christianity. In Corinthians, we extend our hand to grasp our privileges in Christ. In 2nd Corinthians, we open our hearts to receive the comforts available to us. In Galatians, we stand on our feet in the liberty provided by Christ.

When we walk hand in hand with the Holy Spirit, we neither rush ahead nor lag behind. There are nine graces outlined: three toward God (love, joy, peace) and three toward others (long-suffering, gentleness, goodness).

Three toward yourself: faith, meekness, temperance. In the Epistle, we enter the Holy of Holies. God the Father planned it, Jesus the Son paid for it, the Holy Spirit applies it, and we as Christians receive it.

In Ephesians 2, we read about the hope of His calling, the riches of His glory, and the greatness of His power. In Ephesians 1, we see how God worked a plan for the production of His great masterpiece, revealing the nature of man and the walk of a natural man. The greatest proof of Christianity is that it has produced a new man who is approved by God.

Ephesians 4 takes us to the jewel room where we receive our garments of holiness, enabling us to walk humbly with all lowliness and meekness, lovingly enduring with long-suffering, and forbearing one another in love. We walk in peace, diligently striving to maintain the unity of the Spirit in the bond of peace.

At Calvary is where each piece of armor is fitted. We thank God for the finished work on the cross at Calvary. I am grateful that Jesus knew what to do on Calvary that Friday from 12 to 3. He paid the price in full, and there's no charge from now until He returns. When He does return, He will bring greater blessings for us, rewarding us for being good and faithful servants.

If we simply follow Jesus's commandments, we will be standing ready for His return, knowing that He rewards the righteous for their faithfulness. As His Word says, the righteous are not forsaken, nor are their descendants begging for bread.

When God says something, why not take it at face value and walk in faith? We cannot outdo God, no matter what. It's amusing how some think their limited knowledge, acquired perhaps after passing second grade, qualifies them to control the world. God does not need us to intervene in His well-designed Earth or anything else.

I recall my youthful arrogance, thinking I had what it takes to run the world as I walked down the school hallway. But I soon learned otherwise and had to go back to the drawing board. No matter how smart one may consider themselves, they will never know everything. Knowledge must be put into practice; otherwise, one might conclude that two plus two equals five. Take Moses, for instance, who was faithful in all his responsibilities. Moses is renowned as the Lawgiver, ascending Mt. Sinai to receive the Law and then delivering it to the people. However, it's crucial to remember that God is the ultimate giver and maker of the Law. Similarly, Christ is depicted as the Son over His own household.

Throughout history, from Moses to John to Ezekiel, God inspired men to write His Holy Word. It is our duty to uphold every word of it with precision and reverence. God grants individuals the authority to proclaim His holy and righteous Word. Consider how Moses encountered God at the burning bush, Abraham's journey began with God's promise of land, Ezekiel witnessed God's power in the valley of dry bones, and Isaiah received his calling in the year King Uzziah died.

Daniel's journey commenced as he beheld the four beasts rising from the sea, while John's revelation unfolded under the guidance of God concerning Jesus Christ. Even going back to the Old Testament, we see how Adam's relationship with God began amidst the repercussions of sin. That challenge was left on the table for us to address until Jesus went out on Mount Calvary and completed the finished work so that we could be freed from this burden of sin. From Adam to John, no one was deemed worthy to stand for humanity's sins; not even the priests could bridge the gap.

I am thankful to God for Jesus, who made it all clear to the Father that He would stand between humanity and sin. What a mighty God we serve, to relinquish His royal crown for me. Consider the wonderful creation of man by God. From head to feet, it's as if heaven touches earth, while from arm to arm, it stretches out like the horizon—a perfect symbol of the Cross. We can see how God carried man, with a cloud by day and fire by night. Now, we see how Jesus carried us on His shoulders to the cross.

Just imagine if God had not saved Adam from his sin; what would the world look like today? We would all be living in sin forever. As we observe today's world, especially with our young people, it's evident that they need God to guide their paths.

Young people often desire everything handed to them, like at Burger King, where they want it their way. I hope that somewhere in this book, there will be something to challenge their thinking and help them grasp the realities of life.

The older men should guide the younger men on how to navigate through life, and the older women should instruct the younger women to prepare for the challenges of the world ahead. Satan's aim is to lead them astray, knowing his time is short, and he seeks to ensnare as many as possible.

To the young people, I say: prioritize education and make the most of opportunities because the world offers only hardship or a grave if you succumb to its traps. However, be wary of falling into Satan's snares, as he plays by no rules. Invite Jesus into your life for a fresh perspective, seeking His grace and mercy to cover you.

Jesus promised to stand at the door and knock; if you invite Him in, He will be with you. There's everything to gain and nothing to lose. God won't force you to choose Him; instead, He grants you the freedom to decide. The choice lies with you, so seize the moment while there's still time. Yesterday is gone, and we stand at the threshold of tomorrow, facing the future with open hearts.

Someday, I envision a future where all mankind joins hands and echoes the sentiments of the late Dr. King, expressing gratitude for the freedom we now enjoy. My hope is that, before my time on this Earth concludes, I witness humanity united, singing songs of faith and resilience, acknowledging how far we've come together.

With open arms, God beckons us, offering rest to all who labor. A wise individual understands the importance of building on a solid foundation, ensuring resilience against the winds of time. Without a sturdy foundation rooted in God, life's challenges can easily erode our strength.

Yet, in His divine protection since the beginning of time, we find solace from life's chilling winds. We must trust in God's unwavering nature—He is the Great I AM of the Old Testament and remains consistent throughout time in the New Testament. The Old Testament lays the groundwork through prophecy, while the New Testament fulfills the promises yet to come.

If we never get a clear understanding of what is being said in the Old Testament, then we will never have a clue of what the New Testament will present. God laid out His plan from the outset, entrusted it to Jesus for fulfillment, and then passed it on to the Holy Spirit to guide and teach us until His return.

God's flawless plan, crafted from the beginning, is a magnificent masterpiece—without error, perfected from its inception. Jesus is currently constructing the celestial city of New Jerusalem, where peace reigns supreme and violence is nonexistent. I eagerly anticipate the day when we no longer need to glance over our shoulders in fear.

To enter this divine abode, we must intimately know Jesus. God secured the building permit, Jesus possesses the expertise to construct, and the Holy Spirit oversees the project, ensuring it progresses smoothly and peacefully in accordance with divine order.

The world is divided into two parts: day and night. Similarly, the Spirit comprises three parts: Father, Son, and Holy Spirit. The Father spoke all things into order, and the only creation specifically made was man.

Man was fashioned in the very image of God, each piece serving a distinct purpose and designed meticulously. Each part possesses its own name and function, incapable of being interchanged with another part of the body.

The beauty of man lies in his perfect design, each piece measuring 144 cubits and fitting together flawlessly. We must express gratitude to God for crafting such a flawless masterpiece in man. Following this creation, man was placed into a deep sleep, and from a piece taken away, woman was formed to serve as his helpmate. Man should always be appreciative of God's transformation from a pile of dirt into such an awe-inspiring creation.

God had a special plan to communicate with man long before the Earth was formed. Some individuals believe that God's act of creating them is solely to impress them by pulling them from a pile of dirt.

However, God intentionally chose the lowest part of the earth to create man, emphasizing his uniqueness. Man may speculate that God could have fashioned him as a giant, beating his chest like an ape, but God's design reflects his deliberate and perfect plan.

Man should exercise great caution in his dealings with God, as events can unfold whether he is awake or asleep. Regardless of our preferences, God remains in complete control, and we are no match for His authority. At times, God surely finds amusement in observing our earthly endeavors, wondering when we will grasp the truth.

I have always contemplated what would occur if God were to withdraw the air we breathe. Without it, we would resemble fish out of water, gasping for breath until we succumb. Despite this reality, humans often trivialize such matters, acting as though they hold the reins of control.

God will never allow humans to obliterate His creation, although we inevitably face consequences for our actions. Regrettably, we humans are prone to making quite a mess of things from time to time. Instead of assuming responsibility, we often blame God for our shortcomings, conveniently overlooking our own choices.

Rather than faulting God, we need to thank Him for seeing the bigger picture. It's like looking at a dirty window; some individuals foolishly demand a free banquet and then blame God when it isn't provided. Instead, we should take initiative, moving forward without hindering others' progress. Our time on Earth is brief, intended for aligning everything harmoniously, connecting the dots of existence. God doesn't desire for us to remain idle, expecting blessings without exerting effort.

John 14 reminds us not to let our hearts be troubled, as Jesus promises to return for us so that we may be with Him. Reflecting on my youth, I recall hearing my parents speak of God, although it seemed distant and incomprehensible at the time. However, as I matured, I realized the necessity of a guiding force to navigate life's journey. Choosing Jesus as my anchor was a pivotal decision, steering me away from stagnation and uncertainty. Despite Satan's attempts to ensnare me, God's protective embrace shielded me from harm.

Satan relentlessly seeks to lead us astray, employing various tactics to drive a wedge between us and Jesus. Let us not allow anything to obscure the truth, for Jesus proclaimed Himself as the Way, the Truth, and the Life— the sole path to God. Israel's history serves as a cautionary tale, highlighting the consequences of disregarding God's guidance in favor of human folly.

Attempting to deceive God is a futile endeavor, as He sees through every scheme and plan. It is unwise to provoke the wrath of a disappointed God, as Israel learned to their detriment. Therefore, let us remain steadfast in our faith, heeding the words of the Lord and avoiding the pitfalls of disobedience.

I wouldn't trade this remarkable journey I'm on for anything, despite its occasional bumps along the road. Each step is enriched with new revelations from above, lightening the burden along the way. Satan may be displeased with me for putting him in the crossfire and offering him a taste of his own medicine. He's reluctant to swallow his own poison, preferring to dish it out instead.

I ask God to shield me behind His mountain, where the harsh winds of life cannot reach. He's capable of all things without fail. As this earthly life nears its end, I find solace in the promise of a new body that will never tire, unlike this weary vessel weathered by life's storms.

Through it all, I cling steadfastly to God's unwavering hand, whether in the depths of the valley or atop the highest peak. He is the Lily of the Valley, the radiant guiding light. God has bestowed His favor upon me, assuring me of His eternal presence. He has promised never to abandon nor forsake me. Life is fleeting, like a whisper or a small bubble on a vast pond, here today and gone tomorrow.

In my youth, I was curious about the inner workings of the world, pondering what propelled its motion and the forces behind its existence. Little did I realize then that God was the ultimate orchestrator, firmly in control of it all. My young mind was consumed with questions about the who, what, where, why, and when of it all. However, those around me seemed just as puzzled, leaving me in a perplexing state of uncertainty. Nevertheless, I persisted in my quest for answers. The preacher's words resonated with me, emphasizing that God is indeed sovereign and offers solace to those burdened by life's trials.

Then I prayed to the Lord, asking for the light from the lighthouse to shine upon me. Soon after, I heard the preacher inquire, "Have you been to the water? Is your name on high?" This stirred something new within me, signaling the start of a transformative journey. When God lays His hands upon you, your life is forever changed. He touched me and brought wholeness, flooding my soul with joy, ushering in a profound sense of renewal. When God speaks, it's essential to open your ears and heed His words. Some may mistakenly believe that God owes them the world, but in reality, God owes humanity nothing. My hope is that people will relinquish control and allow God to guide them to a place of everlasting peace—a place free from chaos, violence, addiction, and all other hindrances to true harmony.

As I navigate through the complexities of life in this urban landscape, I tread carefully, mindful of the traps Satan has set to ensnare unsuspecting souls. He cares little for how he captures you; as long as you're under his influence, that's all that matters to him.

Satan's snares ensnare the rich, the poor, and those who believe they can outwit him. He relishes the opportunity to demonstrate that human cunning is no match for his schemes. Yet, when Satan rebelled against God in heaven, seeking more power, he was swiftly defeated, for he underestimated the might of God.

Satan may be mighty, but God is almighty—there are no slip-ups in God's plan. While Satan may have thought himself significant in Heaven, he was merely a small fish in a vast ocean. When God pulled the plug and let the water out of his little tank, it became evident that no one can outsmart God, no matter how hard they try.

People often believe they can escape consequences, but eventually, they must face the music. There's nothing free in life; everything comes with a price. Whether you pay now or pay later, the cost of life must be accounted for.

In my early years, I embarked on a quest for truth, seeking to understand the origins of existence. As I progressed, I began to piece together my findings, realizing their potential significance for the future. I documented my thoughts, sensing they held keys to unlocking greater understanding. The culmination of my journey resulted in a book titled "In Search Of," serving as a foundational work for subsequent endeavors. This book expanded my knowledge and deepened my comprehension, placing God at the forefront of my exploration.

Recognizing God's sovereignty as Creator of all things, I entrusted my pursuits to His guidance. With the assurance of His eventual return for His church, I remained committed to further research, seeking fulfillment and peace of mind in the pursuit of truth.

I titled the second book "Peace And Happiness," with the theme centered on Behold He's Coming, reminding us of His imminent return. This book has opened eyes to this theme, offering a broader perspective on life.

Returning to the drawing board, I crafted another book titled "Living In A Dying Land." We indeed reside in a world tainted by sin, but God's plan ensures that our departure from this realm leads to eternal life, where death holds no sway. I will persist in writing until I hear the words "well done, come and receive your reward." The book I am currently writing will resonate across mountaintops and echo in valleys, bringing life, hope, and joy to all who read it.

Reflecting on the numerical sequence of this year, starting as 01-01-23 and ending as 12-31-23, emphasizes a sense of order and continuity. Preparation for writing requires a clear mind, ensuring all mental faculties are engaged. My hope is that my writings bring happiness and clarity to readers. I aim to illuminate minds, fostering clear comprehension of the content. May readers allow their hearts to guide them, avoiding the pitfalls of overthinking.

Satan seeks to cloud minds and sow confusion, but we must resist his influence. By banding together, we can counter his schemes and diminish his impact. Some may passively observe rather than actively contribute to solutions, but such inaction only perpetuates problems. Satan thrives on chaos and ignorance, exploiting confusion to further his agenda. However, we must not succumb to his tactics. He resents God's authority and seeks to undermine His plan, but he is restrained by divine decree.

Judgment begins at the House of Prayer, where the preacher plays a pivotal role. It is the preacher's responsibility to guide the flock and prepare them for the coming of Jesus. Ultimately, the preacher will be held accountable for their stewardship of this sacred duty.

The preacher's role on Earth is to minister to both believers and non-believers, as there is no need for preaching in Heaven. Upon entering Heaven, the Holy Spirit will no longer be necessary, as we will hear directly from Jesus Christ.

It would be unfortunate for preachers to miss their mark. Each of us shapes our own legacy through our actions, so it's crucial not to leave important work unfinished. When Jesus speaks of standing at the door and knocking, He refers to the door of our hearts. We must remain open to His message and not let Satan obstruct our spiritual hearing.

Though Satan knows he cannot ultimately triumph, he still strives to put up a formidable fight. Similarly, some people may persist in error despite knowing better. Surrendering to God's will instead of trying to play the role of a skeptic leads to the right path. Humanity has inherited Adam's sinful nature, ingrained in our very DNA due to his disobedience to God's commands. Straying from God's path puts us at risk of falling into sin.

In life, we have only one opportunity to make the right choices. It's essential to stay within God's protection rather than subject ourselves to unnecessary harm. Some individuals struggle to see the bigger picture due to their preoccupation with trivial matters.

I am writing this book to be a light in a dark world. We require the Word of God to penetrate through this darkness, illuminating the path like a lighthouse. Satan thrives in darkness, as it allows him to operate with greater efficacy. Indeed, darkness is his preferred domain, and he is the prince of this realm.

Satan executes his schemes most effectively in the dark, which is why we must seek the guiding light of God to thwart his deceptions. Keep your spiritual lamp burning bright to fend off the Devil and cultivate a renewed mind to discern when Satan attempts to manipulate your thoughts.

We must be equipped and prepared to combat evil, with the Bible serving as our powerful weapon. This divine weapon contains sixty-six bullets of truth. The initial thirty-nine bullets set the target, while the remaining twenty-seven bring about victory.

God is the creator of this special weapon, intended for every individual regardless of age or ethnicity. Acquiring this weapon requires no identification or payment; it is freely available to all who seek it. There's no need for formal training at a shooting range; the Bible's manual outlines its usage clearly. God entrusted this weapon to His Son Jesus, who passed it to the angels, and eventually, it was conveyed to John, who recorded it for us.

God designed this tool to ensure humanity's guidance, but it's up to individuals to heed its instructions. God's will is for none to be lost, but those who stray from His Word risk losing their way. It's wise for those who have veered off course to return to the right path but continuing on the wrong road is folly.

If we adhere to the Master's plan with wisdom, we can avoid falling into Satan's clutches. Satan eagerly awaits any misstep, hoping to gain control over us and assert ownership. He seeks to weaken us, intending to declare victory with a countdown to our downfall.

Satan employs deceit in every endeavor, prioritizing victory regardless of the cost. He lacks genuine companionship and is solely focused on achieving his goals, often using manipulation to convince us that we owe him something in return for his assistance.

Despite feigning worship at the cradle of Jesus, Satan harbored ulterior motives. It's important to approach situations with discernment, recognizing Satan's deceptive tactics and accepting reality as it is. He strives to obscure his tricks from our awareness, attempting to slip past us unnoticed.

Satan's strategy with Adam and Eve illustrates his cunning nature. Though unable to directly influence Adam, he deceived Eve with a deceptive pitch, leading to their disobedience and subsequent consequences. Disobedience carries a steep price, a lesson learned through their stubbornness and the ensuing repercussions.

"AT THE CRADLE"

What happened at the cradle was beyond what I could comprehend. But I can say God has smiled upon me.

"OLD OIL LAMP"

This old lamp was used for way of light. God said that He would be a lamp unto my feet, and a light unto my path.

Thanks to God for being that lamp, and the light unto my future.

"THE OLD WASHING MACHINE"

We had to get water from the well or go to the spring for water to wash clothes. Things were very hard back in those days, but God made a way for us.

"THE OLD MEAT GRINDER"

This grinder was used to grind up meat for hamburgers.

"FLOUR SHAKER"

This sifter will separate the flour from the wheat germ by turning the crank handle.

"OLD FASHION PERK COFFEE POT"

"CLOTHES LINE PROP"

This prop was used to keep the clothes from dragging on the ground.

Back in those days, people traded different things to help each other. Money was out of the question, but still everyone was happy in a way because the people look up to God to get them through the next day. We had plenty of food. We would trade some things and sell some things for a few dollars.

Some have asked the question, "Would you live in those conditions again?" I hit the brakes and pondered, acknowledging it as quite a significant question. Personally, I don't think I'd choose to go back to those days. However, I refrain from saying "never," as the future holds uncertainties. In today's world, anyone could find themselves just one paycheck away from financial hardship. Therefore, we must be cautious about speaking ill of others.

It's important to remember that God keeps a record of all our words and actions. Some may never have experienced financial struggles, but it's essential to empathize with those who have. Those who have endured hardships without excessive worry have often lived longer lives.

But those who constantly complain about their circumstances and bemoan their financial situation often end up leaving everything behind for others to prosper and enjoy. It's quite foolish to hoard wealth and laugh at the thought of leaving it all for someone else to enjoy.

Every day, I pray to God to keep me grounded and prevent me from losing control. Sometimes, Satan tries to tempt us with whispers of indulgence, urging us to do whatever we want without consequence. But does he truly believe that God isn't watching?

Money certainly has its benefits, but it's not the ultimate solution to life's challenges. Wisdom, on the other hand, is the true key to success. It can take you further than any amount of wealth ever could.

In my youth, I dreamed of having abundant wealth so I could indulge in every desire. However, as I grew older, I realized that my aspirations were leading me down a dangerous path. I began to see how obsession with money could corrupt my life. That realization prompted a positive change in my perspective.

The best course of action is to align ourselves with Commander Jesus Christ, ensuring that everything operates smoothly like a well-oiled machine. When we're able to recognize mistakes before it's too late, we can confidently affirm that we're on the right path. If our mouths start working faster than our brains, we risk short-circuiting, which can lead to trouble. Sometimes, it's necessary to disconnect and allow our thoughts to recalibrate.

How many people are willing to pause their speech to reevaluate their thoughts? It's my hope that readers take this message to heart and give it serious consideration, as we shouldn't take these matters lightly. It's essential to send Satan a clear message: give up and retreat to the dark abyss awaiting you.

"AVIATION PILOT"

During those times, many people struggled financially, resorting to bartering to make ends meet. The 1930s and 1940s were challenging eras marked by scarcity and hardship. Employment opportunities were scarce, but communities united in prayer, seeking divine blessings for sustenance. Although food was available, money was scarce, akin to searching for chickens with gold teeth—an impossible task given that chickens lack teeth.

People of that era embraced a culture of mutual assistance, devoid of the rampant theft and violence seen today. Doors remained unlocked, and car keys were often left in the ignition—a gesture of trust unthinkable in today's world, where theft is rampant. The societal fabric was woven with greater camaraderie and neighborliness than seen today. Unfortunately, drug abuse has permeated both younger and older demographics, eroding social cohesion and personal responsibility.

Satan has seemingly unleashed societal constraints, allowing individuals to run wild without regard for consequences. It's imperative for individuals to introspect and assess how they can rectify their course. While God urges us to pause, observe, and heed His guidance, Satan advocates for blind adherence to his schemes, promising to resolve all issues—a deception that ensnares those who succumb to it.

I believe that today, many young people may find themselves stranded on the side of the highway due to following the misleading influences of Satan. Consider this analogy: placing the wagon before the horse renders it immovable without the horse's power. Do not allow Satan to disrupt your connection with God; it's the same as facing a fierce storm head-on. Some individuals underestimate God's authority, behaving as though Satan holds sway. Such a mindset constitutes a grave error. While God grants life, Satan seeks to extinguish it. If that were not the case, God might have allowed Satan to remain in Heaven. However, God's omniscience prompted Him to assert control over all things.

Playing games with God is unwise, as the consequences are far from favorable. God has bestowed upon humanity the freedom to choose—no excuses remain. When the time for accountability arrives, individuals must face the consequences of their choices. Man has been given clear instructions through the wisdom of the Bible, leaving him no excuse but to accept or reject its teachings; there are no gray areas. Satan's tricks come in many colors, enticing people with bright and shiny distractions.

While I may not have dotted every "i" or crossed every "t," I am confident that I am close to the mark when the roll is called. The Word tells me that only a few will enter, so there's still much work to be done.

Life can be made easier by living according to the right principles and letting God fight our battles for us. When we try to face giants on our own, we often stumble, as we are not equipped for such battles. Instead, we should stand still and watch salvation unfold, trusting in the victory that God will provide.

"CERTIFICATES"

HION COOK STOVE"

"DEGREES"

Andersonville Baptist Seminary

Founded in 1981

Camilla  Georgia

hereby confers upon

William H. Epps

the degree

Bachelor of Biblical Studies

together with all the rights, privileges, and honors appertaining thereunto
in consideration of the satisfactory completion of the prescribed studies and
other requirements.

In Testimony Whereof, the seal of the Seminary and signatures as
authorized by the Board of Trustees are hereunto affixed in the city of
Camilla, Georgia. Given at Camilla, Georgia in the year of our Lord
Two Thousand this first day of September

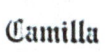

_____
Academic Review Committee Member

John J. Noessa Th.D
Academic Review Committee Member

_____
L Hayes, Th.D
President

Andersonville Baptist Seminary

Founded in 1981

Camilla  Georgia

hereby confers upon

William Henry Epps

the degree

Master of Biblical Studies

together with all the rights, privileges, and honors appertaining thereunto
in consideration of the satisfactory completion of the prescribed studies and
other requirements.

In Testimony Whereof, the seal of the Seminary and the signatures as authorized
by the Board of Trustees are hereunto affixed in the city of Camilla, Georgia.
Given at Camilla, Georgia in the year of our Lord

Two Thousand One
this month of July.

Cheryl Harper
Registrar

Ralph Hayes Th.D.
President

Andersonville Baptist Seminary

Founded in 1981

Camilla  Georgia

hereby confers upon

William Henry Epps

the degree

Doctor of Religious Education

together with all the rights, privileges, and honors appertaining thereunto
in consideration of the satisfactory completion of the prescribed studies and
other requirements.

In Testimony Whereof, the seal of the Seminary and the signatures as authorized
by the Board of Trustees are hereunto affixed in the city of Camilla, Georgia.
Given at Camilla, Georgia in the year of our Lord

Two Thousand Two
this month of February.

Cheryl Harper
Registrar

Ralph Hayes Th.D.
President

"W EPPS TRANSPORT"

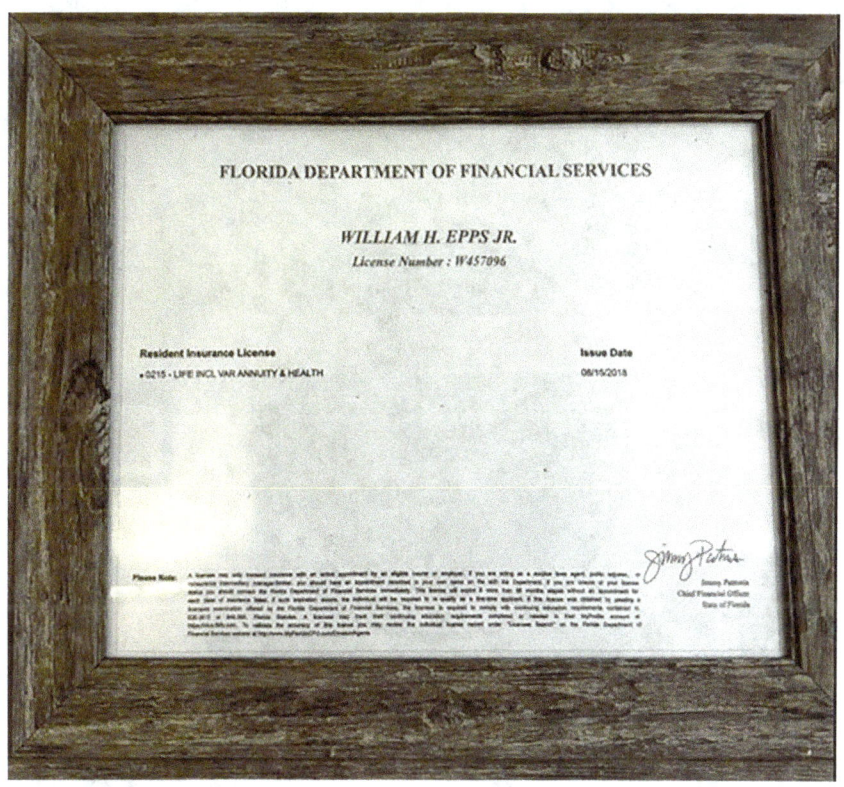

In the Garden of Eden, Satan introduced just one word into the mix: "NOT." That single word caused Adam to falter, convincing him that he wouldn't die but would instead become like one of them. Throughout the Old Testament, Satan stirred up trouble, but he took it a step further in the New Testament, directly confronting Jesus. It seems he had a few loose bolts to confront Jesus so boldly. Knowing he couldn't directly influence Adam, Satan focused his efforts on Eve, seeing her as a more susceptible target. He gambled his last marbles on her, banking on her vulnerability to his deceitful tactics. While God communicated with Adam, Satan whispered soft words into Eve's ear, sowing seeds of doubt and temptation.

History repeats itself, and people today still fall for the same tricks that Satan used ages ago. He will continue to influence until the return of Jesus. Satan is elusive, adept at changing his appearance and tactics. If he didn't, he wouldn't be as effective at deceiving. He keeps himself veiled, making it difficult for us to see his true nature. His pride caused him to swell up like popcorn, but this led to his downfall due to his arrogance. Pride has brought many down, counting them out one by one. Since his fall, he has been resentful towards both God and man.

His ego inflated his chest so much that it covered his ears, leading him to believe he had everything from the start. Sometimes, falling short of the finish line occurs because we aren't always ready at the starting line. We often fail to wait for the signal to start, jumping ahead without listening to the instructions from the Commander.

When you close your ears to the voice of God, you're heading for trouble, and I mean significant trouble. Some people find themselves a few bricks short of a full load, not fully prepared for what lies ahead.

Many choose to remain at ground level, like chickens, assuming their mindset is on par with the eagles. Instead, I suggest putting all your trust in Jesus. He will provide you with the answers you seek. As Paul once said, when he was a child, he spoke as a child, but when he grew up, he put away childish things.

Let's maintain that mindset and bring it to the forefront of our lives. Life is too precious to waste, so make every minute count. Give life great meaning, as God never disclosed how much time we'll have on this Earth. We'll remain here until God says our work is done.

"ART WORK"

Life has plenty of things to offer, and common knowledge can be gleaned from books, provided you have a common understanding of what you're reading. My goal is to write as many books as possible to disseminate basic knowledge among the people, allowing them to partake in the full course of what's being offered. Life is shaped by our choices, so first, we must understand what we want.

Then, we need to comprehend the why, when, where, and how. Afterward, we must establish common ground to integrate these elements. These four aspects form the foundation of how it all began. Once the ground rules are laid out, it becomes easier to follow through and complete the puzzle. The Bible is like a vast puzzle with many pieces. You need to know where to start and how to navigate through it to reach the end.

God has given us an opportunity to see how many pieces of the puzzle we can complete. It's not about who can do the most pieces or who can do it the fastest. It's about persevering until the end. Those who endure until the end will receive great rewards, becoming children of God, hearing the words "Well done." To accomplish and fulfill the tasks assigned to us, we must focus our minds on the leadership of God. Once we understand the how and when, completing the where and why becomes easier.

By following the footsteps of our Commander, Lord Jesus Christ, our deeds will be recorded in the heavenly roll book as well done on Earth, despite its sinful nature. For those who have been faithful with a few things on Earth, there awaits a greater reward in heaven. I can attest that God has shown favor upon me throughout the years; He has been exceedingly good to me. Having run the race for Jesus for a long time, I am still standing strong. Just keep your hand in the hand of Jesus, and He will see you through.

Some may think Jesus owes them something, but the price has already been paid in full on that hill called Calvary, during the hours between noon and three pm on what we call Good Friday. It was good because only Jesus could accomplish such a feat, shedding His blood for the sins of humanity.

"ART WORK"

"ART WORK"

"CONCLUSION"

I hope that the words I said will bring great joy and happiness to the readers who has taken this book to be a part of their collections. This book combines both the Old Testament and the New Testament. My hope is that it will enlighten readers and elevate them to a new level in their lives.

I aspire for my books to spread joy and happiness to every corner of the earth. Knowing that people appreciate my work would bring me great peace of mind. I welcome feedback from readers to gauge their thoughts on my writing. As long as God grants me the ability to write, I will continue to produce transcripts.

God instructed me to go forth and teach His people, as they are perishing due to a lack of knowledge. Thus, I heed His command and follow His guidance. I encourage readers to continue exploring my books, with the hope that they will gain a clearer understanding through them.

Yours Truly,

Dr. William Epps

From the Cradle to the Present

Author: William Epps Jr.
Rating: Gold

"...a heartfelt memoir that intertwines personal reflections with spiritual insights, showcasing a life journey guided by faith and wisdom."

In "From the Cradle to the Present," Dr. William Epps shares a profound journey through his life, intertwined with spiritual insights and biblical teachings. The book serves as a memoir and a guide, offering a unique blend of personal experiences and spiritual wisdom.

Epps's narrative begins with his early years, where he balances his studies with teaching Christian Education, and his aspiration to learn how to fly airplanes. His journey through life is marked by perseverance, as he overcomes various challenges and continues to pursue his passions, including art and aviation.

Throughout the book, Epps delves into biblical teachings, drawing lessons from the Old and New Testaments. He emphasizes the importance of faith, wisdom, and obedience to God's commands, and he reflects on the significance of Jesus's sacrifice for humanity's salvation. Epps's appreciation for the beauty of God's creation and his emphasis on resisting temptation are recurrent themes that resonate deeply.

The book is rich in biblical teachings, emphasizing the importance of wisdom, the role of Jesus Christ, the significance of the Sabbath, and the power of faith. Epps shares his spiritual insights and the transformative impact of living according to God's principles.

Epps's ability to blend autobiography with spiritual guidance makes "From the Cradle to the Present" not just a memoir but a source of inspiration. The book encourages readers to reflect on their life paths and seek wisdom in the teachings of the Bible.

"From the Cradle to the Present" by Dr. William Epps is a remarkable book that earns a Gold rating for its comprehensive exploration of life's journey, viewed through the lens of faith and spirituality. The author skillfully blends personal experiences with deep biblical teachings, providing a guide for navigating life's challenges with wisdom and resilience. As a self-help book, it excels in offering practical advice for personal growth, self-reflection, and leading a meaningful life.

Dr. Epps's honest reflections and spiritual insights serve as a source of inspiration and motivation, making this book an invaluable resource for anyone looking to deepen their understanding of faith and its impact on personal development. In conclusion, this book is highly recommended for those seeking to explore the intricate relationship between personal experiences and spiritual beliefs.

–   *Greg P. of MainSpring Books*

www.ingramcontent.com/pod-product-compliance
Lightning Source LLC
Chambersburg PA
CBHW060352130626
46553CB00003B/1202